THE FUNDAMENTALS OF
SAFE GUN
HANDLING

Understanding the Dynamics of Pistols

Kevin Grant, DBA, MBA, BSc
PRACTICAL PISTOL TRAINER

Pensiero Press

The Fundamentals of Safe Gun Handling:
Understanding the Dynamics of Pistols

Pensiero Press

http://www.PensieroPress.com

Books are available through Pensiero Press at special discounts for bulk purchases for the purpose of sales promotion, seminar attendance, or educational purposes. Special volumes can be created for specific purposes and to organizational specifications. Please contact us for further details.

Copyright © 2023 by Pensiero Press

ISBN: 979-8-9893555-4-9

*Kindle and electronic versions available

Cover and interior: Gary Rosenberg • www.thebookcouple.com

10   9   8   7   6   5   4   3   2   1

CONTENTS

DEDICATION

I dedicate this book to all athletes who represent the industry of competitive shooting.

There are many individuals who consider firearms as tools that inflict harm. In reality, anything can cause harm once utilized in a manner to do so. Understanding how to safely use firearms is important. This book is a basic guide to the fundamentals of safe gun handling and the dynamics of pistols.

FOREWORD
THEORY INTO PRACTICE

by Ronald Brown

Safety is important in all aspects of sport. Understanding the tools that we use is vital. Some sports are more dangerous than others, but all sports rely on the basic principles of safety. In this competitive environment, there is need to reiterate the safety rules and the understanding of how to handle pistols efficiently.

I have been in many situations on the gun range where competitors were disqualified for their unsafe firearm handling. I have also seen veteran competitors being unsafe with regards to the handling of their firearms.

As a practical pistol trainer and competitor, I urge my students to refresh themselves with regards to the fundamentals. I too at times relate to the practical and theoretical aspects of safe gun handling to ensure that I am effectively manipulating the firearm when in use.

I have known the author of this book for many years. We travelled to many regions and competed in many competitions together. I assisted him with his training programmes and coached him with regards to practical pistol. He is very dedicated to the progress and achievements of others and is devoted to the development of the sport.

I guarantee that Kevin's wealth of knowledge in the sport of practical shooting, and the experience he gained over the years as offered through this book, will help him pass along information to those who wish to further develop themselves and those who wish to start in the sport.

ACKNOWLEDGMENTS

This book is written in acknowledgment of the pistol owners, sports persons competing in regional and international competitions, and all the individuals who want to understand the dynamics and components of a pistol.

I want to also acknowledge the efforts of the persons listed below in assisting me in the development and publishing of this book.

Dr. Cheryl Lentz, *The Academic Entrepreneur*, keynote speaker, international best-selling author, TEDx Speaker, top professional quoted on: ABC, CBS, NBC, and Fox.

Mrs. Kristin Grant, Grant Attorneys at Law PLL.

Mr. Richard Durant, Practical Pistol Trainer, International Range Officer.

Mr. Ronald Brown, Practical Pistol Trainer, Grand Master, Dragon Shooting Solutions.

The images in the book are owned by me or used with express permission of Practical Pistol Shooters throughout the Caribbean region.

Special thanks to all who assisted me with regards to this book.

OVERVIEW

These safety rules have been established to ensure the safety of those individuals who use and have access to firearms.

The use of firearms is an inherently dangerous activity. Your activities and actions must always be conducted in a manner that consistently safeguards yourself and others against harm or injury, and property against damage and destruction. These rules must be adhered to protect the lives and safety of all and preserve your privilege to continue life with your loved ones.

Handguns have been used throughout the centuries in many athletic disciplines. This book relates to two pistol types: the revolver and the semi-automatic pistol. Using pistols are fun, once used in a safe manner. Understanding the safety rules prior to using a pistol is important. Different athletic shooting disciplines require different types of pistols. Sporting athletes must know what type of equipment is needed for their respective competition. Doing research and test firing various pistols will give you the opportunity to find a pistol that best suits you.

Firearms must be licensed by the Commissioner of Police in Barbados or the Commissioner of Police in your respective region. Use of firearms without a valid license will result in fine or imprisonment. This book is intended to teach licensed firearm holders and registered shooting range club members around the world, the logistics surrounding firearms and safe firearm handling. It is the user's responsibility to obey all applicable laws with respect to the use, ownership, purchase, or possession of firearms.

Remember, a firearm is only dangerous when used unsafely.

SAFETY

Core Safety Rules

1. **Muzzle Discipline:** Always keep the gun muzzle pointed in a safe direction.

2. **Firearm Operation:** Always keep the firearm unloaded until ready to use.

3. **Trigger Finger:** Always keep your finger away from the trigger until ready to shoot.

Other Safety Rules

1. Always know your target and what is beyond.

2. Always make sure your firearm is safe to operate.

3. Never use a firearm while under the influence of a drug.

4. Store firearms in places not accessible by unauthorized persons.

5. Use the correct ammunition for the firearm.

Equipment Required (by *all* shooters on the range)

- Safety Glasses

- Ear Defenders

- Enclosed Shoes

- Sleeved Shirts

Firearms, Ammunition, and Equipment
are the Tools.
The Mind is the WEAPON.

CHAPTER 1.
STANCE AND GRIP

Stance and Grip

- A stable platform from which to fire fast and accurately at multiple or moving targets.

- Balanced, flexible, and mobile.

Isosceles Stance

- Squarely face the target

- Arms and elbows slightly bent

- Feet shoulder width apart

- Two-handed grip applying pressure with both hands

- Forms an isosceles triangle with the body and the arms outstretched

- Body weight over the balls of the feet

Weaver Stance

- Angled (side on) to the target

- Shooting arm angled across the body-arms slightly bent (weaver) or shooting arm locked out (modified weaver)

- Support arm elbow is bent and angled down

- Two-handed grip applies push/pull pressure

Grip

Established in the Holster

- Holster grip = shooting grip

- Initial "V" adjustment

- Barrel in the line with forearm

- Adjust for proper trigger finger placement

- Strong, consistent grip

Hand High on Back Strap

- Increases control and reduces felt recoil

- Too High: Interface with action or cause injuries

- Too Low: Increased muzzle flip while firing

Two-Handed Grip

- Use two hands wherever possible.

- Provides the best control.

- Correct support hand grip: Meaty portion of the support-hand thumb high into the remaining open grip panel.

- Support-hand index finger touches the bottom of the trigger guard.

Thumbs

- Do not exert pressure against the frame or you may unintentionally release the magazine while firing.

- Thumbs should not interface with the cycle of operation.

    Do not place strong-hand thumb under the support hand—this pulls the support hand away from the grip panel.

Strength of Grip

- Shooting hand pressure is front to back

- Shooting hand is a "firm handshake"

- Must be able to isolate trigger finger

- Support hand pressure is side-to-side. Hold as tightly as possible without causing a tremor.

- If shooter is "readjusting" between shots, grip is not tight enough.

CHAPTER 2.
SHOOTING FUNDAMENTALS

To shoot any firearm accurately, there are certain fundamentals that must be applied. These fundamentals are aiming, breathing, grip, trigger control, and follow through.

These fundamentals can be applied in different ways depending on the type of firearm being used.

Aiming

Dominant eye

Similar to your dominant hand everyone has a dominant eye. To locate your dominant eye focus on an object with both eyes open. Extend your arms forward, bringing them together to  form a triangle in the center, and then place that object in the center of the triangle.

Bring your hands a few inches to your face while keeping the object in view. When your hands are a few inches from your face, they should be in front of the dominant eye.

Aiming consists of two things: sight alignment and sight picture.

Sight Alignment

Sight alignment is the relationship between the front sight and back sight. The front sight and back sight must be in alignment and there must be even space on both sides as seen in the illustration below.

incorrect   incorrect   correct

Sight Picture

Placement of Sight Alignment on the Target

- Front sight in focus

- Rear sight blurred

- Target more blurred

Trigger Control

Movement of the Trigger Until the Gun Fires Without Disturbing the Sights

- Finger placement between tip and first joint of trigger finger

- Trigger finger moving independently

- No frame contact with trigger finger

- Pulling straight back prevents pushing muzzle to the left when firing

- Increase and decrease of pressure

- "Let" the gun fire surprise you

- Maintain trigger contact between shots

*The two most important fundamentals in pistol shooting are Sight Alignment and Trigger Control. (They must be applied simultaneously.)

Breathing

- Increases oxygen in the bloodstream

- Strengthens muscles

- Clears the vision

- Aids in concentration

Use of Breathing Control

- In close quarters NOT important.

- Aids shot placement at longer distances or for more precise shots.

- Shoot during the natural respiratory pause (breathe in, out, pause, then shoot).

Follow-Through

All Fundamentals Must Be Maintained Until the Bullet has Left the Muzzle, Instantly SETTING-UP the Next Shot

- Re-set trigger.

- Maintain intense focus on the front sight throughout recoil and recovery.

- Re-acquire target (it may have moved).

- Call your shot.

Mental Discipline Required for the Best Application of the Fundamentals

- Self-confidence, positive thinking, and self-control.

- Know that you can WIN.

- Be certain your students know they can WIN.

CHAPTER 3.
PISTOL HANDLING

Handling Techniques

- Drawing

- Loading and unloading

- Holstering

- Clearing stoppages

- Techniques for fast and safe use of firearm

- Left- and right-hand utilization

Basic Steps to the Draw From Holster

Firearm Grip

- Grip

- Draw

- Two hands

- Lock

Drawing Considerations

The five-step draw. Step two is divided into two steps: lift the gun out of the holster and then drop the elbow, bringing gun to belt level position.

- Always start with holster secured.

- Common drawing mistakes:
    - ✗ Muzzle covering body
    - ✗ Bowling
    - ✗ Anti-aircraft
    - ✗ Excessive body movement (bending, dipping)
    - ✗ Discus-throw

Drawing Speed

- First: Build a safe, correct, smooth draw.

- Once the draw is mastered, draw combat speed every time: "Draw like you mean it."

- Practice – Practice – Practice.

Holstering

Always Done Reluctantly

- Once out, keep it out.

- NO speed requirement.

Involves Three Activities

1. Down and Scan Format

- After immediate threat is over.

- Muzzle DOWN to ready position (decocked, safety, trigger finger discipline).

- SCAN for other threats and break tunnel vision.

2. Think

- Reload?

- Malfunction?

- Visually check the handgun's condition.

- Get ready for the next encounter.

3. Re-holster

- From the ready position—reserve the draw steps.

- Two safety checks.

- Accomplish one-handed.

- If two hands are required, do not muzzle your support hand as you holster.

Loading the Semi-Automatic Pistol

- Two safety checks

- Insert magazine

- Chamber cartridge

- Holster pistol—Ensure that all safety aspects of the firearm are engaged, i.e., safety on for single action or decocked for double action when holstering.

Unloading the Semi-Automatic Pistol

- Two safety checks

- Remove the magazine

- EJECT chambered cartridge and lock the slide open—do not catch

- Physical and visual inspection of empty chamber

- Secure and store

CHAPTER 4.
PISTOL MECHANICS AND OPERATION

All firearms fundamentally operate in the same manner whereas a trigger is squeezed causing the hammer to engage the firing pin.

Although firearms operate in a similar manner, they carry different components based on their functionality.

All firearms carry a **frame, action,** and a **barrel**. The action determines how the gun operates and it is a collection of parts that enables the gun to fire.

Other components of a firearm are as follows:

Trigger—This component releases a spring powered hammer or striker to fire the cartridge.

Slide—This component has multiple functions. The slide is made up of multiple components. It houses the firing pin as well as the extractor. It cocks the hammer to the rear and ejects the cartridge from the firearm.

Hammer—This component engages the firing pin, which contacts the cartridge primer.

Magazine release—This component, when activated, releases the magazine from the frame.

Barrel

CHAMBER   LOCKING LUGS

NOZZLE

FEEDRAMP

Inside of the Barrel

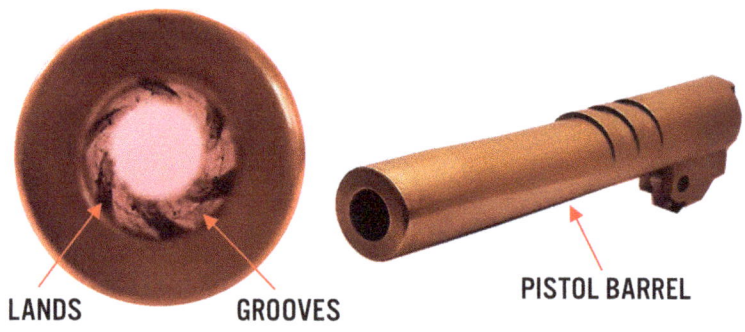

LANDS   GROOVES

PISTOL BARREL

Rifling—Rifling is important when it comes to accuracy. It is mechanically grooved striations within the bore of the barrel. Rifling is spiraling lands and grooves that engrave the bullet and allows it to spin through the bore. The rifling will determine the velocity and the spin rate of the bullet.

ALWAYS **KEEP THE GUN POINTED IN A SAFE DIRECTION.**

ALWAYS **KEEP YOUR FINGER OFF THE TRIGGER UNTIL READY TO SHOOT.**

ALWAYS **KEEP THE GUN UNLOADED UNTIL READY TO USE.**

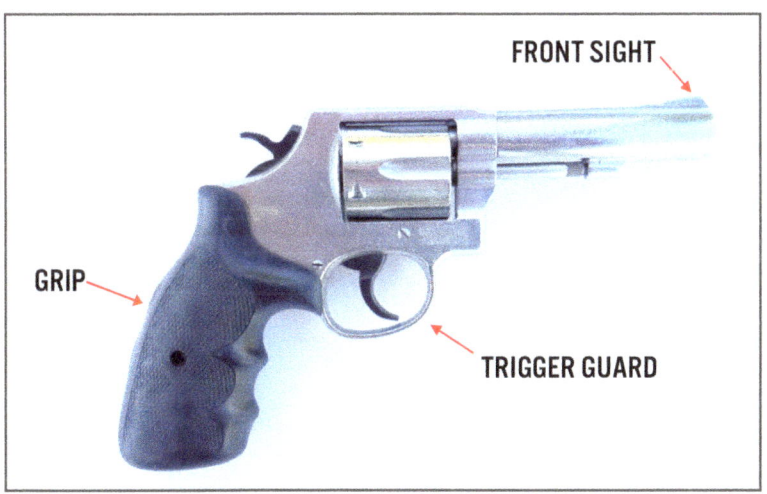

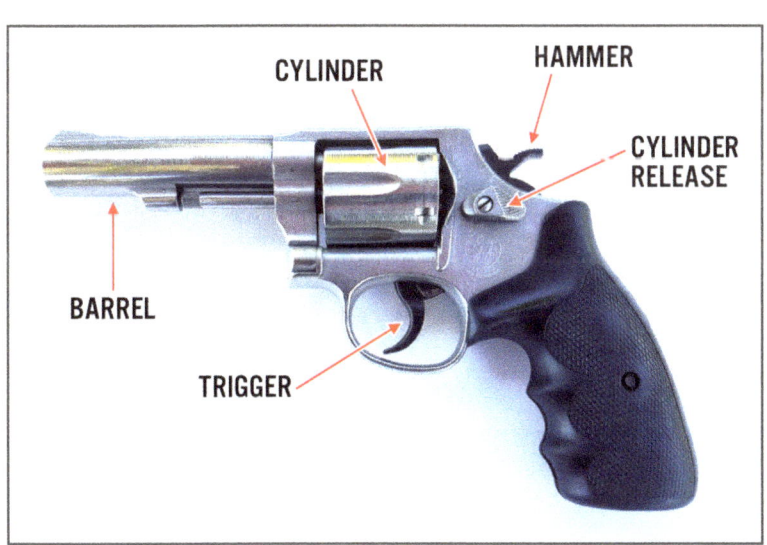

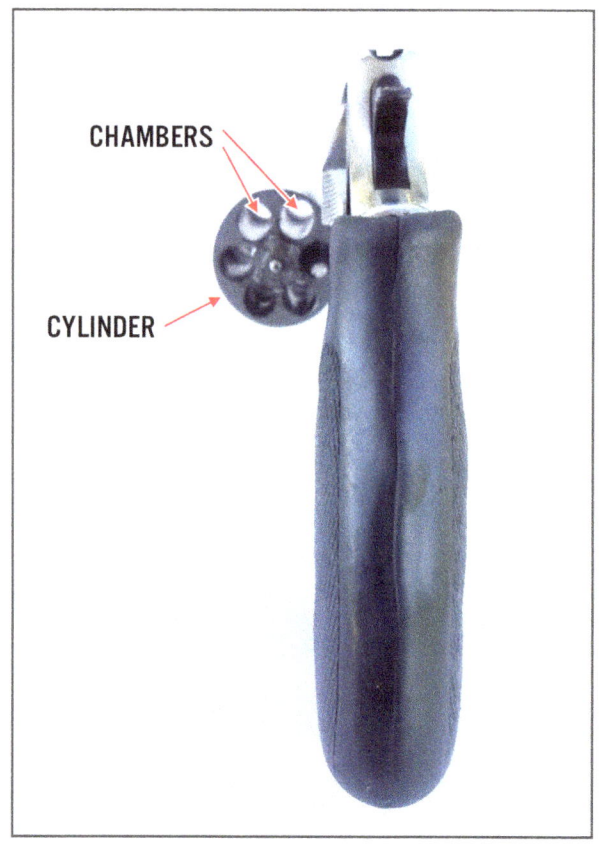

Illustration of a Smith & Wesson .357 magnum (Double Action)

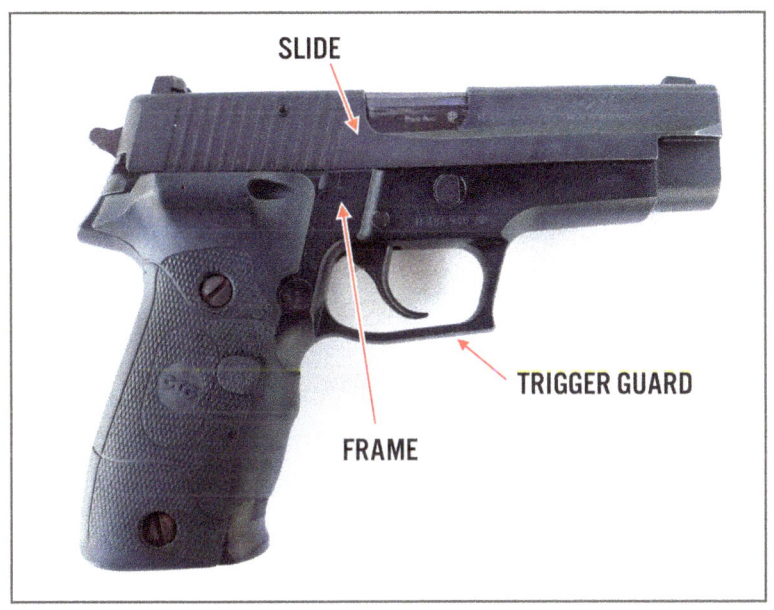

SLIDE

TRIGGER GUARD

FRAME

FRONT SIGHT   BACK SIGHT   HAMMER

SLIDE LOCK

DECOCKER

TRIGGER

MAGAZINE RELEASE

Illustration of a Sig Sauer P226 9mm pistol. (Double Action)

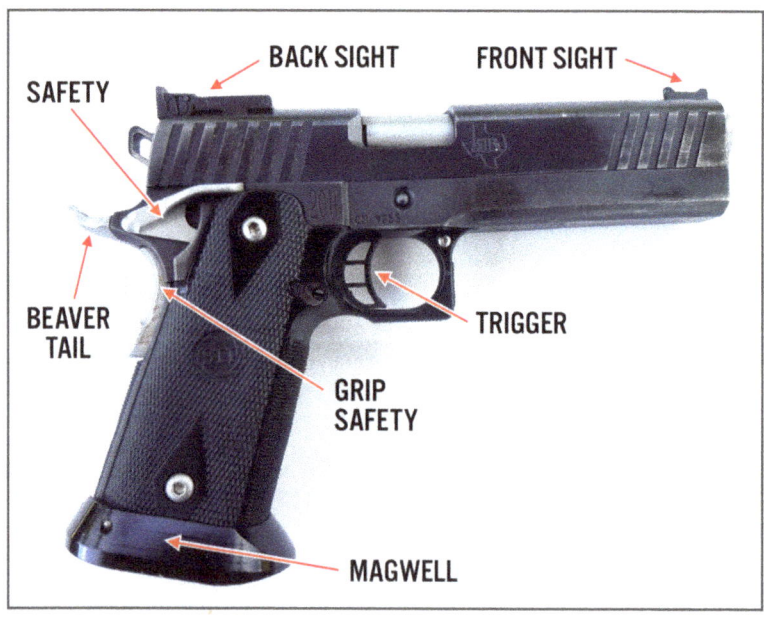

Illustration of a STI EDGE 9mm (Single Action)

There are other types of pistols built for specific shooting disciplines. There is precision shooting and practical pistol shooting. Practical pistol shooting comes in a variety of athletic disciplines including International Defensive Pistol Association (IDPA), United States Pistol Shooting Association (USPSA), and International Pistol Shooting Confederation (IPSC). IPSC and USPSA disciplines of shooting are fast paced and rely on speed, accuracy, and power. The sport consists of a variety of divisions, ranging from standard, revolver, production, production optics to the open division. The IDPA discipline focuses on defensive pistol techniques that simulate real life situations. Illustrated below is an STI Grandmaster .38 super. This firearm will be used in the open division. The previous firearms, such as the Sig Sauer, will be used in production and the STI Edge in the standard division.

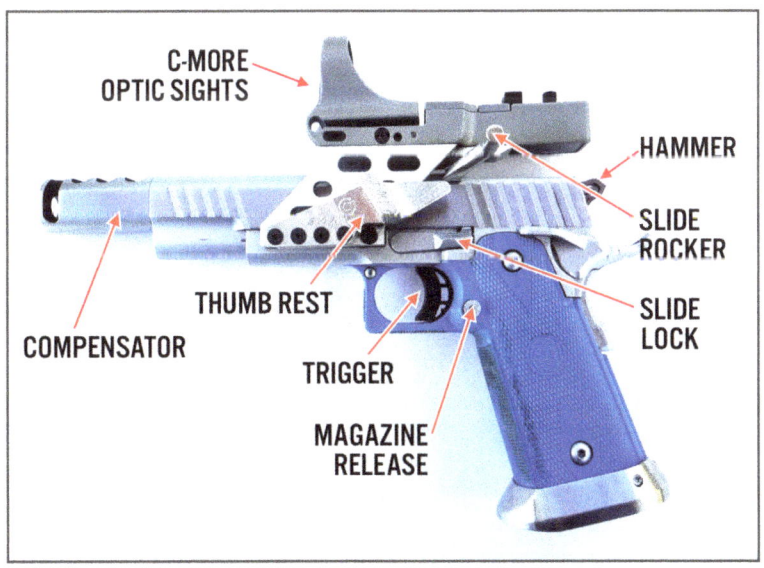

Types of Pistol Actions

Single Action

With a single action pistol, each time the trigger is engaged it performs a single action. The hammer is released when the trigger is engaged. The hammer must be manually cocked for the first shot.

Double Action

Double action pistols perform two actions. The trigger cocks and releases the hammer.

Operation of Semi-automatic Pistol

Most pistols have the same method of operation. Single action and double action operate the same but have slightly different parts. The operation is the same: pull trigger and release the bullet.

Let us look closer at the operations of a pistol.

Firing the Pistol

When the trigger is engaged, it activates a hammer (internal or external) which in turn strikes the firing pin.

Slide Back (Unlocking)

Once the trigger is pressed, the gas operation aspect of the firearm takes effect. The "bang" sends the slide rearward with the assistance of the recoil spring, opening the chamber of the pistol.

Extracting the Bullet

There is a claw shaped device located in the slide of the pistol. This grabs the rim of the cartridge and pulls the cartridge to the rearward position. This occurs during the slide back (unlocking phase).

Ejection of the Bullet

When the cartridge is extracted to the rear, it connects with a pointy object called an ejector. The shell hits the ejector and is thrown out of the slide (action) via the ejection port.

Cocking

When the slide goes to the rearward position, it cocks the hammer (striker) and readies it for the next shot.

Feeding

When the slide (action) reaches its rearward limit, it is propelled forward. The forward motion strips a cartridge from the magazine and pushes that cartridge onto the feed ramp of the barrel and seats it into the chamber.

Slide Forward (Locking)

This occurs when the pistol reaches its normal state and the slide has come to a complete stop and fits snug on the frame.

CHAPTER 5.

AMMUNITION

Ammunition

There are various types of ammunition. Ammunition is selected based on its use. A lot of focus is paid on firearms, but ammunition is just as important. There are various cartridge types including **rimfire** and **centerfire** cartridges.

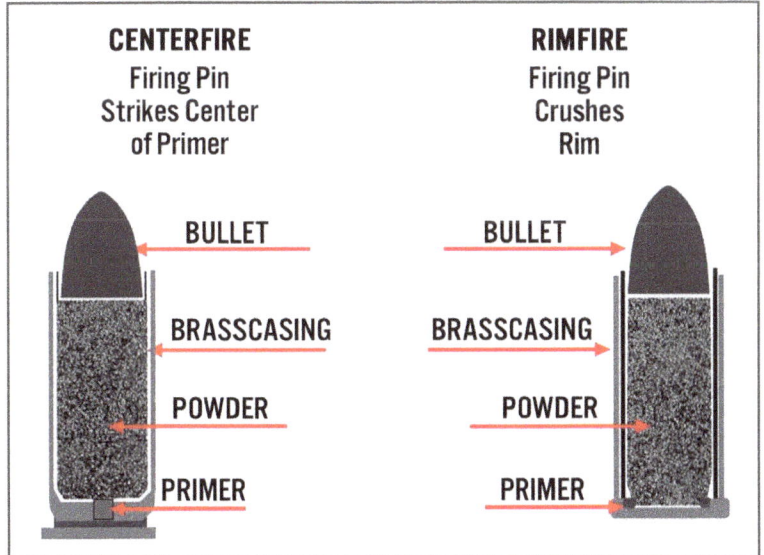

Rimfire—Mostly in .22 caliber, rimfire cartridge has the primer seated on the rim of cartridge.

Centerfire—Centerfire comes in a variety of calibers.

Unlike the rim fire cartridge, a centerfire cartridge keeps the priming compound in the center of the cartridge.

Cartridge Components

Cartridges have four components.

1. **The case**—This houses all other components. It is generally made of brass but can be made of steel. The centerfire cartridge case contains a primer pocket that holds the primer.

2. **Powder**—This is a chemical compound packed inside the case of the cartridge. Once this powder is ignited, gases are created, and the bullet is propelled from the nozzle. This is made primarily of nitrocellulose and nitroglycerin. When the powder is ignited, it creates high pressure gases that build up in the case and forces the bullet out of the casing.

3. **Bullet**—Bullets have a variety of shapes and sizes. They can come in lead or copper. They can come as hollow points or full leather jackets.

4. **Primer**—The primer creates a spark that ignites the powder. It is in a small metal cup containing a pressure sensitive priming compound.

Firing Sequence

When the trigger is squeezed the following takes place: The hammer strikes the firing pin. The firing pin hits the primer on the cartridge. The powder is ignited inside the case creating high pressure gases that force the bullet out of the cartridge.

Cartridge Firing Sequence (see diagram on next page)

1. Cartridge placed in the chamber.

2. Firing pin strikes the primer or case rim and ignites the priming compound.

3. A flame is generated inside of the cartridge and burns the priming compound.

4. High pressure gases are created due to the burning of the priming compound.

5. The gases push the bullet through the bore and an explosion "BANG" is heard.

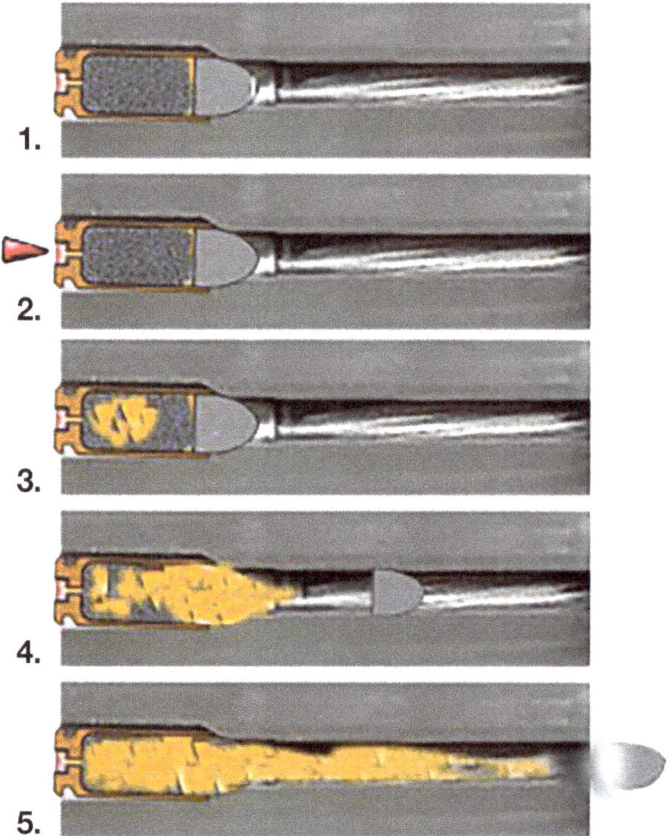

1.

2.

3.

4.

5.

Ammunition Types

Ammunition can be identified by looking at the ammunition box or by looking underneath the cartridge. Cartridges are labelled with the ammunition type stamped at
the bottom.

Some ammunition is loaded to higher pressures and
can create greater damage on impact to the target. Des-
ignation +P or +P+ will be seen on the cartridge of this

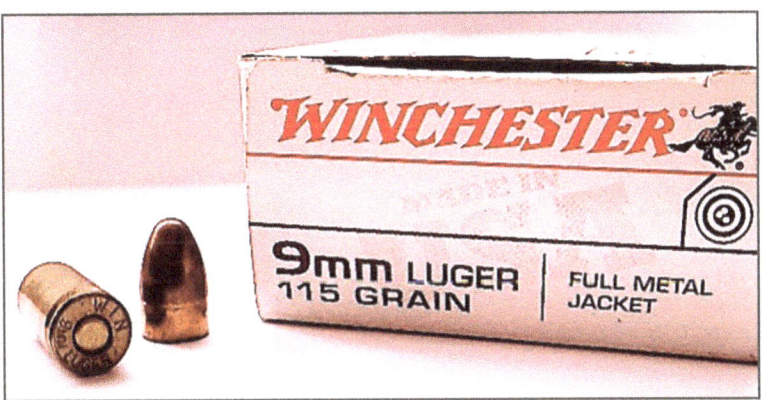

particular type of ammunition. While +P refers to ammunition that is loaded to higher pressures, +P+ are loaded to even higher pressures than +P and can only be used in firearms built to fire ammunition at those pressures. For example, you can find 9mm at +P or at +P+.

Guns that are not made to fire high pressure ammunition can be destroyed or wear and tear faster because there are not suited for that type of ammunition. Ammunition should be stored in a cool, dry place. Ammunition which has been soiled or exposed to solvents or liquids should not be fired.

Cartridge Malfunctions

There are three major types of malfunctions that occur in a firearm.

Misfire—This is a failure of the cartridge to ignite when the primer has been struck by the firing pin.

Hang fire—This occurs when there is a delay in the ignition of the cartridge once it is struck by the firing pin. One cannot tell if it is a hang fire or a misfire and because of this the firearm must always be kept pointed in a safe direction. If this occurs wait 30 seconds before attempting to open the action on the pistol.

Squib load—A squib load occurs when a cartridge develops less than normal velocity or pressure when the primer is struck. This can damage a firearm as the bullet may not leave the barrel and may be lodged inside of the bore. When a squib load occurs, there can be reduced recoil, reduced noise, or reduced muzzle flash.

CHAPTER 6.
TARGETS

There are various types of targets used in sports shooting. The selection of targets depends on the sporting discipline. Targets have different scoring zones.

Targets have the scoring zones written on them. If a shot hits the scoring ring on the target, it is given the higher score. The illustration below shows a shot landing on the scoring line. This shot will be given the greater score.

A shot that lands on the scoring line will be given the greater score.

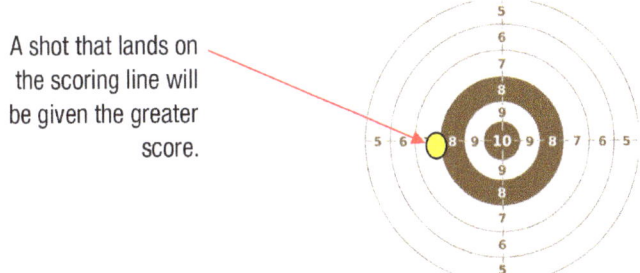

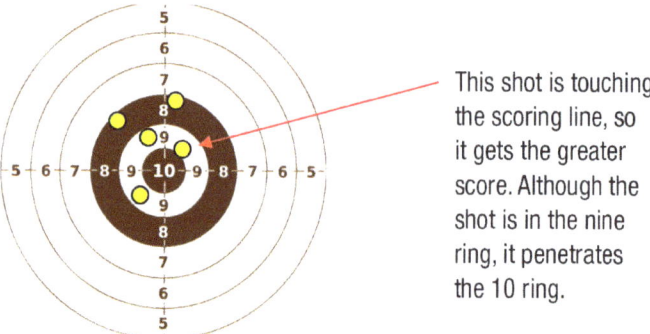

This shot is touching the scoring line, so it gets the greater score. Although the shot is in the nine ring, it penetrates the 10 ring.

There are five shots on the above target depicted in yellow. This target scores 10, 9, 8, 7, 6, 5 from the center ring being 10, to the outer ring being six. Scoring this target is a matter of simple mathematics.

(8 x 2 shots) + (9 x 2 shots) + (10 x 1 shot) = 44 points

CHAPTER 7.
PISTOL SELECTION

Selecting the correct firearm is especially important. There are various types of pistols built for specific reasons. When selecting a pistol, one should do research first. Speak to firearm dealers, go to the range, and speak to experience firearm handlers.

Here are some reasons that you will consider when going to purchase a firearm.

- The size of the firearm. (You do not want to buy a concealed carry firearm as it is too bulky. Not only will it be seen, but the weight may affect your health in later years.)

- Cost of the firearm.

- Type of firearm (double action vs. single action).

- How the firearm fits in your hand. (If you have small hands, you may want to purchase a small frame firearm.)

- Availability of parts. (Do not purchase a firearm that you cannot obtain parts for easily.)

- Availability of ammunition. (Do not purchase a firearm that you cannot obtain ammunition for easily.)

- Is this a licensed firearm's dealer? (Ensure you purchase a firearm from a reputable **LICENSED** dealer.)

Reasons for Owning a Pistol

Below are some reasons for owning a pistol

- **Hunting**—People hunt birds, monkeys, ducks etc.

- **Sporting**—Athletes compete in various disciplines of pistol shooting in hopes of excelling to the top of their class.

- **Self-defense**—An individual may desire owing a firearm for personal protection (this can be in the form of protecting property, family, or person.

- **Collection**—One may want to become a firearms collector.

REMEMBER: Acquiring any type of firearm requires that you complete an application form that *must* be sent to the commissioner of police for their approval *prior* to thinking about accessing or obtaining a firearm. Different jurisdictions have varying regulations. Kindly do your research regarding the laws for your particular region.

GLOSSARY

Action: The "working mechanism" of a firearm that loads, fires, extracts, and ejects a spent cartridge and in some instances reloads a new cartridge.

Airgun: A rifle or pistol which a projectile is propelled by means of compresses air.

Backstop: A device constructed to stop or redirect bullets fired on a range.

Baffles: Barriers to contain bullets and to reduce, redirect or suppress sound waves. Baffles are placed either overhead, alongside or at ground level to restrict or interrupt errant or off-the-target shots.

Ballistics: The study of what happens to moving projectiles in the barrel and in the flight—their trajectory, force, impact, and penetration. The study is divided into three sections: internal, external, and terminal. "Internal" refers to what happens inside the barrel before the bullet or shot leaves the muzzle. "External" is what happens after the bullet or shot leaves the barrel and travels to its final point of impact. "Terminal" relates to the behaviour of a projectile when it strikes its intended target while transferring kinetic energy to the target.

Barrel: The metal tube of a gun made from iron or steel through which the bullet or shot charge passes when a gun is fired.

Berm: An embankment used for restricting bullets to a given area or as a dividing wall between ranges.

Breech: The rear end of the barrel. In modern firearms, the portion of the barrel into the cartridge is inserted (also referred to as the chamber).

Bullet: A single projectile fired from a firearm.

Bullet trap: A device designed to trap or capture the entire bullet and fragments as opposed to the redirecting and the projectile into a water or sand pit.

Caliber: Internal diameter of a gun barrel or the external diameter of a bullet or shell.

Cartridge: A self-contained unitized round of ammunition made up of a case, primer, powder, and a bullet. The case is usually made from brass but may be steel metal alloy or plastic.

Course of fire: A Rifle or Pistol Match being shot.

Discipline: A means of enforcing rules, including procedure, penalties, and administrative processes.

Energy: The amount of work done by a bullet, expressed in foot pounds.

Firearm: A term used to describe any gun, usually small, from which a bullet is propelled by means of hot gasses generated by burning powder.

Firing distance: The distance between the firing line and the target line.

Firing line: A line parallel to the targets from where firearms are discharged.

Firing position (Point): An area directly behind the firing line having a specified width and depth occupied by a shooter, their equipment, and if appropriate, an instructor or coach.

Firing range: A facility designed for the purpose of providing a place on which to discharge firearms.

Gun: An instrument that uses a propelling charge to move a projectile. For the purposes of this document, the term includes both firearms and airguns.

Handgun: A slang term used to describe pistols, either auto-loading, single shot, or cylinder types held in one or two hands with no other support, such as shoulder stock, etc.

HOT range: A "HOT" range is one where firearms are currently being shot. When a range is declared "HOT," it means that users of the range may be firing.

Impact area: That area in a backstop or bullet trapped directly behind the target where bullets are expected to impact.

Line of sight: An imaginary straight line from the eye through the sights of a gun to the target.

Machine gun: A firearm which fires more than one cartridge when the trigger is pulsed only once.

Magazine: The part of a repeating firearm which holds cartridges in position ready to be loaded one at a time into the chamber. The magazine may be an integral part of a firearm, or a separate device attached to the action.

Misfire: Failure of a cartridge to discharge after a firearm's firing pin has struck the primer.

Muzzle: The forward end of the barrel where the bullet exits the firearm.

Muzzle energy: The energy of a bullet as it emerges from the muzzle. (Usually expressed in foot pounds.)

Penetration: The distance travelled by a projectile from the point of impact in each media to its final stopping point.

Pistol: A firearm capable of being held, aimed, and fired with one hand. Also known as a revolver or a handgun.

Range: The distance travelled by a projectile from the firearm to the final impact point. Three terms apply to range: "point blank," "effective," and "extreme." Point blank range refers to distance less than five yards; effective range means the greatest distance a projectile will travel with accuracy; extreme range the maximum distance a projectile will travel. Term also refers to the facility designated for the purpose of shooting at regulation targets.

Revolver: A type of pistol equipped with a cylinder that consists of several chambers, each containing a cartridge or loading components.

Rifle: A modern firearm designed to be fired from the shoulder. Its main characteristic is a rifled (grooved) barrel that imparts a spin to a single projectile as it travels through the bore. Some rifles designed for military and law enforcement use may have a pistol grip stock in addition to or instead of a shoulder stock.

Rules and regulations: Standards used in the operation of a shooting range. Rules and regulations are set up to govern the method of range operation to include health and safety. The violation of the rules and regulations generally carries penalties enforced by operational personnel.

Safety baffles: vertical or sloping barriers designed to prevent a projectile from traveling into an undesired area or direction. Most often used to prevent bullet from leaving the range proper.

Shotgun: A firearm designed to be fired from the shoulder with a smoothbore barrel that fires shot shells possessing a varying number of pellets. Some barrels are designed to be used with rifled slugs, and the barrel may be rifled. Some shotguns designed for military or law enforcement may have pistol grip in addition to or instead of a shoulder stock.

Shot shell: A cartridge, designed to be used in shotguns. A unitized round of ammunition in comprised of a hull or shell, a primer, powder, wad, and shot. Cartridges are normally constructed from plastic or paper.

Small arms: Firearms that may be both carried and discharged by one person, as opposed to artillery pieces. Small arms are not subject to precise definitions, but the term usually includes rifles, handguns (pistols), shotguns, submachine guns, and machine guns.

Trajectory: The path a projectile travel from the muzzle to the point of impact.

Trap: A device or machine used to launch targets in the air or on the ground. Usually used in sporting clays and skeet shooting.

SPECIAL THANKS

I want to thank my parents for always being there to support me through my endeavours. Many thanks to my father who introduced me to pistol shooting and taught me the basics of safe gun handling. I want to thank my wife and kids who are always pushing me to further develop myself.

Dr. Cheryl Lentz needs special thanks, as she guided me on my journey as an author and was instrumental in my progress.

To my friends and colleagues, thank you.

ABOUT THE AUTHOR

Dr. Kevin Grant is the Operations Manager at the Academy of Sport, University of the West Indies, Cave Hill campus. Before working at the University of the West Indies, he worked at Ernst & Young as a senior auditor. Dr. Grant completed his Bachelor of Science in Business from the University of Phoenix in 2008. He was then enrolled in the University of Wales, where he completed his Master of Business Administration (MBA) in 2011. Dr. Grant joined the University of the West Indies in 2013 with a focus of becoming a professor in the field of management and leadership.

As Operations Manager, he is responsible for strategic planning and the development of effective systems and processes within the Academy of Sport. Dr. Grant is always keen on self-development and in sharing knowledge and expertise with his peers. To further develop his skills, he enrolled as a student at Walden University and completed his Doctor of Business Administration (DBA) in 2019. As Alumni of Walden University, Dr. Grant sits as a member of the National Society of Leadership and Success, offering expertise in management and leadership strategies to various organizations. Dr. Grant has published six chapters and four eBooks on leadership concepts. The latest is *The Effect of Ethical Leadership on Employee Engagement: A Moral Approach to Management* (2023). He received #1 Best-seller and #1 International best-seller for his chapters published in doctoral anthology series: *The Refractive Thinker*®.

To reach **Dr. Kevin Grant** for additional information or guest speaking, please contact him at **e-mail: kevin grant26@gmail.com**

ABOUT THE PISTOL ATHLETE

Dr. Grant represents the Barbados region as an active practical pistol competitor. He competed in various countries such as Ecuador, Jamaica, France, Curacao, Trinidad, and other regional and international territories. As a pistol trainer, he hopes to develop the practical pistol discipline within his region. He is an active member of the International Practical Shooting Confederation and represents the International Range Officer Association. Dr. Grant held numerous courses on the fundamentals of safe gun handling and certified many individuals in the region.

www.ingramcontent.com/pod-product-compliance
Lightning Source LLC
Chambersburg PA
CBHW051557120626
46551CB00013B/1551